MEANING BEYOND REASON

D1712952

ALSO BY ANTHONY CAPONI

Voice From the Mountains: A Memoir
Boulders and Pebbles of Poetry and Prose

MEANING BEYOND REASON

Selected Essays

ജ

Anthony Caponi

ISBN: 978-1-935666-20-2

Cover: Detail of bronze self-portrait by Anthony Caponi
Back cover photo © Jeff Baker

Library of Congress Cataloging-in-Publication Data

Caponi, Anthony.
Meaning beyond reason : selected essays / Anthony Caponi.
p. cm.
Includes bibliographical references and index.
ISBN 978-1-935666-20-2 (alk. paper)
1. Life. I. Title.
BD431.C27 2011
128--dc22

                              2011008734

Nodin Press, LLC
530 North 3rd Street
Suite 120
Minneapolis, MN
55401

Dedicated to my wife Cheryl

CONTENTS

Introduction

All I practice and teach today is the consequence of youthful conditioning in a time and place of relative innocence, where truth and reality owed less to words than active contact with the land and daily living. As such, I am the product of fortunate circumstances.

I was born a peasant among peasants in a remote village of the Apennine Mountains in a poor region of Italy that for centuries was Papal territory, where the Catholic Church still dominated cultural values. Only five years of school was available and considered adequate to educate country folk.

I was born in 1921, when Mussolini came to power and as dictator used schools to indoctrinate children with fascist ideals. Only half a day of school was required. The rest of the time was work and play.

At work we learned practical skills, how to use tools and how to grow food. At play we invented games and made our own toys but mostly we enjoyed the freedom of exploring the outdoors without supervision.

In this simple, innocent world children enjoyed a benign parental neglect that encouraged self-initiative and the good feeling of self-sufficiency. Books were rare in my youth. Then, people told stories and peasants sang ballads while working in the fields. From these simple people I learned that happiness and security are independent of material wealth, and practical wisdom is not something ones learns in the artificial environment of school.

Much later I found that I was one of the under-indulged children that Maria Montessori compared favorably to the overly protected ones from affluent families.

Looking back, I realize how little influence the teaching of the Church and Fascism had on my personal development in comparison to my appreciation for the natural beauty that surrounded my native town.

Unencumbered by too much information, my state of ignorance was an adventure in personal discovery that promised a life of inexhaustible possibilities for creative exploration. In this way I learned a lot before I knew the words for what I knew.

Words could not compete with the monumental reality of a mountain. It was in contemplating nature that I found spiritual fulfillment and the desire to explore other aspects of life.

My dilemma, but also my purpose, in writing this book, is to convey non-verbal insights through the very idiom I consider too prone to self-contradiction and too disposed to serve a lie as well as truth.

I adopt the language of reason to meet the unbeliever half way in rediscovering a more direct method of knowing, by restoring words to their subordinate role of assisting experience, so that experience itself—beauty, love and other rich manifestations of the mind—may rank higher than their explanation; so that knowledge and education may regain human relevance.

*Without plucking a leaf or leaving a body in want
I take from life.
I take all I can and give it all back with a personal flavor.
I rub softness into granite; knead clay to free from it a
form that becomes, with the life it takes.
To give ideas a body, to animate a body with spirit,
I sculpt.
To share the pleasure of transforming the mind's ghosts
into caressable shapes,
I teach.
I teach the unzipping of the inner layer of the mind
where experience ferments and nourishes judgment,
where the soul expands and swells the vents of expression,
flavoring existence with shared feelings.
I teach the fusion of spirit and body, so not to divorce
understanding from the sensuous rewards of knowing.*

Like a tree, man should have his autumn,
a time to shed his summer mantle,
to show the limbs of his aspirations
and the trunk of his basic nature,
rooted in the ground, even as he reaches for the sky.

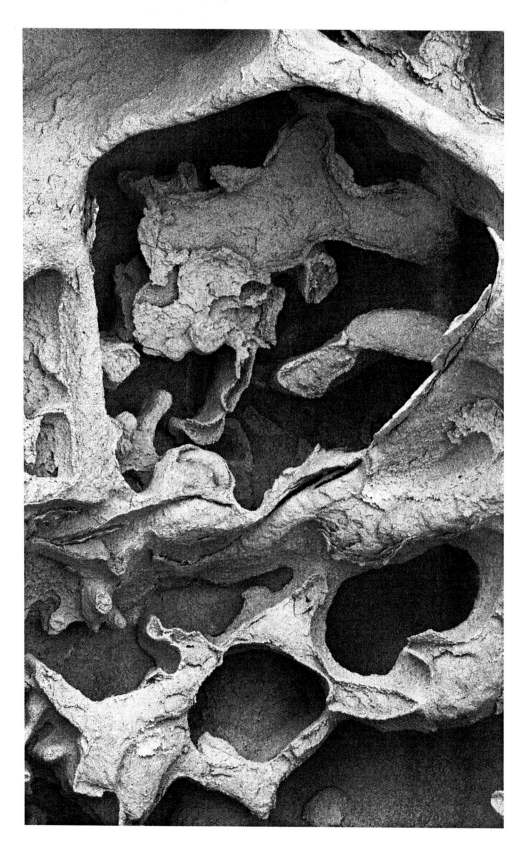

Man and God

So much is said …
what man ought to be.
**Tell me what man is
and I will know
what man ought to be.**

If Adam and Eve lost Eden
for having done one better,
the preacher of sin lost God
by attributing to Satan
what is beautiful and good

Man knew right from wrong before he knew the word sin.
He knew fear and love before either were defined.
He recognized God in all things and freed his spirit
with music and dance before he knew the words to
prayers and songs.
He knew the art of colors and the magic of dreams.
He knew beauty before it had a name.

Early man was one with nature and fully equipped to appreciate the gift of life. What he saw and touched was reality. What he felt and tasted was reward and nourishment for his physical and spiritual well-being.

To him, the beginning and the beyond was mystery and the mystery was God.

Mother Nature, the visible dimension of God, experimented with many life forms before creating man, a creature endowed with the ability to reflect upon the beauty of its world and express appreciation to its maker through music and dance, poetry and songs—the language of art and the human spirit.

These qualities that best distinguish man from other creatures are the complementary sides of his dual nature of builder and destroyer, lover and killer, thinker and believer.

Like other animals, man must feed on other living things to survive. Nature favored man with a cunning mind that placed him at the top of the food chain.

From this vantage point, he was free to cultivate and expand on his spiritual nature. He sought survival through group efforts and found security in human fellowship. This led to the development of language and social order.

The things that rewarded feelings and taste were perpetuated through rituals and social customs. Taboos were placed on food and behavior that did not promote survival and quality of life.

The process of socializing human behavior led to value-judgment—good and bad, right and wrong—and their consequences of reward and punishment, Heaven and Hell.

As language evolved from simple communication to become a complex medium of logical reasoning, it enabled philosophers and scientists to explore and discover every small component of the physical world and human thought.

Reason explained the explainable, but left in an intellectual limbo the main essence of human life—consciousness—the living spirit that energizes our total being; that indivisible sense of the self that we call soul; that inner self that intuitively connects us to something greater than ourselves.

There must be a good reason why nature dispenses life in small packages. There must be a benign purpose for keeping the human creature ignorant of his preexistence and future destiny.

Man is born helpless and ignorant.
He learns the same lessons that his parents had learned, blooms into maturity, then, like a flower, wilts and dies.

Thinking of the unknowable only makes me aware of my ignorance.
But, I am not alarmed by my human shortcomings. I am not bothered because I believe.

I believe because I exist through no efforts of my own.
I know nothing of what I may have done to deserve my present life.

Yes, I believe in "the Son of God" because we all are the sons and daughters of God.

As creatures and creators,
mankind may well be the best, conscious manifestation of God.
As such,
I'd rather believe and trust a mystery beyond human comprehension than have "God" reduced to human dimensions.

Concern for life after death, destiny of the human soul, and definitions of a creator, God, have been a continuous preoccupation of mankind. Man's attempts to define God as a physical and spiritual entity have resulted in many idols and different modes of worship without arriving at a universal concept that would serve all.

Fortunately, the human mind experiences more that it can explain: our appreciative response to the physical world of form and colors, our blissful abandon in love, our spiritual experience in the arts and other human expression, and the intuitive perception that feeds our imagination and connects us to the spiritual essence of what is beyond understanding.

In other words, all honest beliefs and rituals that evoke a spiritual experience are valid and necessary for meaningful living even if they reveal human limitations.

If God is everything, to love anything in the world is to love God.
To live in harmony with the world is to be in harmony with the creator.

Though no human being can intellectually portray or explain God, it has been convenient to make God in the image of man to better fix spiritual concentration on something that speaks our language and understands our pleadings.

Belief in a power beyond human understanding is conditioned from infancy. A child learns to trust a system that provides for his security and well-being. He does not connect parental love with godly providence but as the child matures beyond the narrow circle of dependency, he finds a bigger world to which he belongs. He sees how animals depend on plants, how plants reach out to the sun.

Beyond the sun and beyond the outer limits of human understanding, the child in man still trusts that a divine power is playing a parental role.

In whatever man undertakes, in everything he depicts or describes, be it God, art or nature, he mostly describes himself—his thoughts and aspirations, his need to give free play to his creative imagination.

For most vital needs, man has a corresponding appetite that bypasses reason in its compelling response to satisfy the senses. The rewarding experience of satisfying mind and body sets the basis for taste and moral values.

To assure survival, nature resolved to make living a pleasure.
It is the protection of these pleasures that makes life tenacious.
It is the pursuit of rewarding experiences that compels the mind to be resourceful.
It is the culmination of sensuous rewards that we perceive as beautiful or fulfilling.
It is the aesthetic experience that philosophers call spiritual in the realm of religion and myth that gives unity and scope to life.

Every myth, every imagined bliss of heaven, every horror of hell is a projection of a mundane experience.
Every thought, every human aspiration is a creative reconstruction of one's perception of the world.

From all appearances one can honestly conclude that Heaven and Hell are realities of this world and that every creature begins life in the only paradise known to man.

This conclusion is consistent with the ever-present duality of life in which the good and the bad must coexist to sharpen perception and appreciation of their distinctive qualities.

So it is that life teases the mind with opposing concepts, allowing our free will to choose and organize; to derive satisfaction from the harmony we achieve within ourselves and with the world we live in.
So it is that the more we enjoy our earthly paradise the more we fear its inevitable end.

Nothing less than the spiritual experience we derive from pure appreciation for our gift of life can reassure our human spirit that we are a perpetual part of an orderly creation.

Science can explain the human mind as chemical reactions of firing neurons. It can locate and measure the responses of different components of the brain. It cannot explain or understand the essence of human consciousness—that complete sense of the self commonly referred to as the human soul.

Whatever the chemistry that fuels the belief in God and perpetual life, it is the nonmaterial experience of the sublime that connects us intuitively with the essence of the infinite.

Our mind is all that we are, whether we call it intelligence or soul, but the way we use it determines the depth and quality of our being.

One aspect of the mind is its reasoning power that is usually expressed in words and identified as intelligence.
This dimension of the mind functions as a tool: to resolve problems, to investigate the material world, to discover and utilize the mechanics of natural laws, to advance technology and other practical conveniences of life. The aspect of the mind that recalls and manipulates information is what schools have chosen to educate.

The mind, as a receptacle of all the experience that we have lived, digested, and assimilated into a felt identity, is disposed of as mere emotion, intractable and inapplicable to logical reasoning.

Whatever can be measured, tested, and explained, becomes the objective truth that plays a disproportionate part in contemporary values and education.
All that we know as the summation of what we are—the sublime experience of our felt existence—is commonly referred to as "things of the heart."

This splitting of the mind has promoted false ideals of human enlightenment and robbed too many people of the felt oneness of self-identity.

We are what we feel, what we explain is another thing.

Having concluded that intellect is man's most unique quality, philosophers and teachers downplay his most basic tendency to respond to life with animal feelings.

"It is almost human!" is said of some animals that display human-like behavior, unaware that the word *human* describes the very animal qualities that man distinguishes from his learned, formal behavior.

We are no longer sure whether we are educating man to benefit from his human potential or changing him into a useful instrument of a society beyond his control.

Sociologists find it necessary to study primitive societies, animals and innocent children to rediscover our basic nature. These studies result in a collection of data that enrich the verbal play in academic circles more than they enrich general understanding.

A child is shaped by his physical environment, he learns from what he lives more than from what he hears, he learns more from demonstrated behavior than from what he is told.

It is the irony of our times that simple people and untamed animals may enjoy a greater harmony within themselves and nature than the over-trained and spiritually neutralized individual.

All that man knew and did naturally the psychiatrist rediscovers as remedy—contact with nature and the pleasure of simple labor that combines mind and hands, recreates soul and body in a unified experience.

A healthy mind works in unison and responds to life with feelings.
The apparent separation between thought and felt responses is reinforced by
the very idiom favored by reason—the spoken language.

Words and reason are a good fit. They facilitate communication and are
easily recorded. Even more important is that verbal thinking lends itself to
testing and measurements of how well a person has absorbed information
and how productively he can apply what he has learned.

Using this criterion, what we look for in a human being is not much
different than what we expect from a robot.
We promote usefulness more than personal well-being.

The real qualities of a meaningful life, the qualities of the deeper inner self,
cannot be assessed with standard tests. The better part of our being finds
expression and development in creative activities—the very activities that
are readily dismissed whenever an institution of learning finds it necessary
to reduce its offerings.

What we learn from lectures and demonstrations can be repeated and explained.
What we are can only be expressed.

The ancient story of Eden is a good analogy for the dilemma of the dual aspects of the mind. There man was to choose between the gifts of divine providence or taste the fruit from the forbidden tree of knowledge.

Man chose the power of knowledge in God's laws.

Though the biblical taboo that forbids inquiry into God's laws is too rigid a formula for contemporary man, the basic principle is not lost.
The insipid fruit from the tree of knowledge, in itself, does not nourish the human soul and is not worth losing the rewards of Eden.

So it is that, since recorded time, language and reason have been the major means of inquiry into the mystery of natural laws and life itself.
The culminating irony is that modern science has discovered the human brain has a richer inner life that is not part of conscious behavior and has even less connection with rational thought.

Early man was a nomadic hunter who moved with the game and climate changes before he learned to control his environment.
His domestication of plants and animals was the big step toward a permanent residence and the making of civilization.

He built cities for the glory of man and temples for the glory of the gods.
He structured laws and religion to establish ethics for human behavior.
He imitated God's creation with parallel harmonies in art and music.
Man sought beauty and goodness in himself and in all that God had created.

Then, he opted to challenge God and the spiritual nature of humanity.
He put faith on hold, subject to his rational scrutiny.
Man was to assume nothing that his logic had not confirmed.

The Age of Reason became the age of doubt. The spiritual man became the practical man who used reason to reshape values and his mission in life.
Man became the tool and servant of change. Motion became the sure confirmation of life, with no sense of direction and no place of arrival.

The creature that learned to walk on two feet, to study the sky with an upright ego; the sovereign hunter who recorded his kingdom in the caves of Altamira; the spiritual man, who rendered God in his own image, now diminishes himself to a selfless observer of physical reality and demotes truth to a disarray of disconnected facts.

Through the monocular vision of reason, the universe expands while man and his world shrink. All that was intuitively profound is being resurfaced in shallow waters to smash spiritual tenets against the reefs of reason.
The great nomadic hunter has returned to his nomadic world, where his ambition moves him from place to place, from temporary residence to temporary friends; from temporary family to uncertain loyalties.

This summary of mankind's history is neither the beginning nor the end of an ongoing story.

Man adapts and survives even as civilizations slide from glorious heights, touch bottom and bounce back with renewed vigor.

Adaptability may assure man's survival but it also confirms that man is a very trainable animal.

He relinquishes love and conscience to specialize in the art of killing his own kind.

He submits to teaching and values that stifle the joy of living.

And so we go on searching the unknown with a dual mind that turns on itself by demoting all felt human responses to a lesser dimension of reality.

We listen to philosophers and scientists who cannot agree on a unified principle of life that would reassure a mortal creature that his relative ignorance falls within the scope of a supreme order to which he owes his very existence and a full measure of trust and appreciation.

Gravel Pit of Words

For the person who uses words like so many empty boxes stacked
in the warehouse of his mind, waiting to be filled with meaning,
his harvest will be more words, defined by other words, as empty boxes
fitted within boxes within boxes, until containers become contents and all
content is no more than empty containers.

An ideal grows from the soil of experience,
in the light of wisdom and time,
reaches full bloom, then seeds into
words.
WORDS! That's all there is to an ideal that is not replanted,
by each person in the soil of new experiences.

Words that are not dipped in the juice of experience are sterile seeds in shallow soil. Though such words may connect a chain of thought that links concepts to more complex abstractions, though this phenomenon demonstrates intelligence, the result is mere mechanics—void of flavor and human content.

Words and knowledge are not necessarily close allies.
In art school my teachers were artists without the gift of words to formulate impressive explanations.
They taught by way of inspiring demonstrations.
From them I learned as a person learns in the presence of someone who knows—through example and spiritual osmosis.

I later went to a university where teachers were eloquent speakers, where words were limber from lack of weight and practical experience.
There I learned about the talkers and the doers. The talkers talked about the art that doers had already created, in its self-evident beauty.
The lecturers used the best artistic achievements as a mere point of departure to satisfy their vanity for words. At best they achieved an independent expression with its own rational and aesthetic qualities that had little in common with the aesthetic experience they tried to explain.

As tools of information and mechanical explanation words may achieve their purpose, but to convey meaning and human content words must achieve expression.

There is something wrong in the way words team up with man as obedient servants, become part of his daily experiences and gradually infiltrate his every expression and thought.
There is something wrong when man stops behaving according to his nature and substitutes labels for his senses to determine what is good or safe.
There is something wrong in the way man is becoming dependent and numb while his words acquire freedom, respectability and built-in values.
There is a threat in the fact that words are adaptable perennials while man is perishable.

While words become entrenched in the creases of time, man is born ignorant and helpless. He has only a lifetime to balance the mechanics with the substance of living.

With classroom-practiced eloquence they speak of philosophy and of the mind; universal love and brotherhood. So, students and teacher use noble issues to produce a barricade of words to keep soul and body at intellectual distance.

As knowledge expands beyond the capacity of a single mind, man retreats into the deep ruts of specialization that hide from view the broader dimensions of life.

Specialists accept the consequences of their relative ignorance.
The professor and the doctor defer judgment to the plumber and the mechanic. People talk on all subjects but need lawyers and critics to tell them what is permissible or in good taste.

We are told what to eat and how to dress, how to rear children and how to care for pets, how to make friends and how to have sex. Even then, we fear that what we like may be in bad taste and what we say may be biased or politically incorrect.

Conditioned to ask questions from teachers and specialists, we are losing the ability to be self-sufficient in a world that links individuals by a fine thread of total dependence.

While the accountant determines the correct amount due to the government, and lawyers play the game of verbal skills to determine the relative losses of their clients, the individual has become ever more a bystander with no more to do than claim his freedom to proclaim his freedom, to sustain his illusion of independence.

"Progress" has cornered humanity into an impersonal, institutionalized existence.

From infancy through the better part of maturity man is compelled by law and social pressure to submit his mind and body to mass conformity. Individual family values and parental prerogatives have been supplanted by police and social workers, school principals and doctors, do-gooders and informers.

Because of the efficiency of modern mass communication, no totalitarian government in the past ever achieved a more complete regimentation of the mind than our uniform education system. At no other time in history was man more conditioned to accept the word as the equivalent of reality.

Thus, the universal consensus of right and wrong changed from ethical judgment to its legal definition, too wordy and too complicated to enlighten the average person.

Words all around, words and pollution;
words too worn out to sell cars or bibles,
words of politicians and commentators,
all wanting to make it clear in their own words.

Ask a lawyer...and he will check his books, full of laws, redefining old laws,
full of words and stipulations needing lawyers to read.
Ask a teacher...and he will quote the findings of other authorities on the
subject.
Tell a student...and he will take notes, without lifting his eyes to
acknowledge the teacher.
The student has no time to pause and integrate meaning.
Fearful of losing the words in the fusion of understanding, he lets them float
on the surface of his mind to keep them handy for the quiz.

Truth built on words is easily disassembled by words.

It is a philosopher's pastime to re-argue old ideas, to make of truth a sphere of disagreement rather than a point of convergence. Consistent with the practice of letting half a truth argue with the other, scholars take sides in the perennial verbal sport of disagreeing.

The three concepts deemed essential to human fulfillment—truth, goodness and beauty, fill thick volumes with tiresome explanations, to contradict the principle of simplicity necessary to truth and beauty.

Though understanding is often stranded between intuitive insight and reasoned conclusion, deep in the silent chambers of the mind, a person knows that any two of the above concepts are part of the other.

Some philosophers imply intellectual depth through the questions they pose. "What is the meaning of life?" "Is there a God?" "What am I?" are some of the recurring questions for which they don't expect a definitive answer.

They delight in verbal paradoxes that tease the mind with misapplied logic.

To answer "What am I?" the "I" must become the observer, thus preempting the subject that was to be observed.

I know myself best when creatively occupied and so spiritually involved that life, God and I become one experience.

"What am I?" is usually the beginning of a lie.
Even when I know, words will have their say
and make of my thoughts a verbal play.
When I really am, I am deep in work;
deep in play, or deep in love.
As such, I don't even know my name.
To answer what I am, I must stop being. Part of me
must surface to the shallow regions of the mind.
I must disengage from the experience of knowing,
to become the observer of what I've just stopped being.

Man sees himself through love and labor, as he touches the world of spirit and forms with the ungloved hands of his mind and body, as he lets reality touch him with the weight of mountains and the spirit of open skies, as he views the results of his labor and hears his soul exclaim,
"That, and that, I am!"

If words could convey understanding, beyond simple information and mechanical explanations, years of schooling could be reduced to a fraction of time. The professor could teach all he knows in a few days and make each student his equal.

Information for its own sake, without an inspired soul to engage it creatively, is like sand without the binding cement to make it usable.

One cannot understand from words more than what he already knows or convey more than what he is.
One person's "I like" may mean more than another person's "I love."
A responsible person's "I" may be less self-centered than another's "we."

A given word uttered by different individuals does not have the same power or meaning.

                Your TEN   and   his NET
                              are hardly the same
You say BAD   he says DAB
                    he dips on your answer
5 + 5 = 10.   picks up   .01 and calls it
                              even
                            A   is   A
                  either way You look at it
                              unlesss
                              Yours
    is CAPITAL   and his   a small a
        You agree   and   he agrees
                              but
                  if he could only see
what You see   or You see   what he sees
                  when You think
        agreed   and he thinks   deerga

The vocabulary of the mind is not limited to words.
An art teacher may speak of form, color and space but artists need no verbal basis for their creation. Their visual statement is directed to, and through, the senses to engage body and mind in silent contemplation.

I have taught theories of art and translated the non-verbal process of creative activities. I achieved the psychological distance that permits intellectual detachment from the subject of discussion. In so doing, I was losing the presence of spirit that energized my own work, that very quality of intense being that I expected to teach others.

Having crossed and re-crossed the threshold between doing and explaining, I concluded:

> One may speak of love or eulogize the dead but
> the ones deeply involved rarely talk.

Fortunately, Mozart and like geniuses didn't squander their time explaining their music. Beethoven, even if willing, would not have been literate enough to earn a degree in musicology in today's schools. Yet, the combined efforts of all the scholars of music since Beethoven's times could not produce anything comparable to the sheer strength and spiritual heights of the first few bars of his Fifth Symphony.

Michelangelo, the artist who best embodies the vitality and spirit of the Renaissance, was consumed by a creative passion that brought his humanity and skills in focus to elevate beauty beyond the confines of descriptive realities.

Michelangelo was a humble man often tormented by the discrepancy between his artistic vision and common rationality.
He despaired about his three "unfinished" sculptures, *The Slaves,* that still emerge from the coarse marble that trap and forever burden their naked bodies. Surely the great artist must have sensed that he had achieved something greater than what he had planned when he held back his chisel from the noble figures, each at the same stage of development.
He could not contradict the dictates of his artistic soul while complaining of not fulfilling his stated intention.

Though historians accept Michelangelo's words at face value, his laments echoed the thinking and expectations of his times, that all finished works have a smooth surface.
Michelangelo honestly believed that he never found time to finish the sculptures that we know, today, as among his best.
He had no knowledge of a subconscious mind that supersedes reason and intent when an idea evolves into a richer concept, as modified by the medium and the creative process.
In other words, what Michelangelo said was less true than what his artistic judgment led him to do.

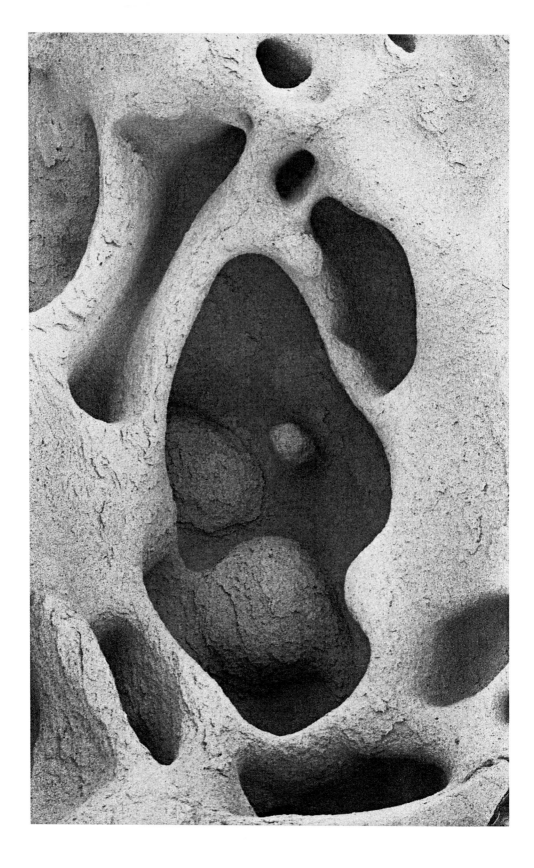

Words That Prefabricate Conclusions

Man invented words then let words prescribe his thoughts, with all the conveniences and limitations inherent in the medium.

The word is a simple abstraction that lends itself to simple statements as well as complex thoughts. Structurally, it is the equivalent of a masonry brick that shapes simple walls or a community of buildings.

Some words represent complex thoughts and values that make them susceptible to distortion as they become burdened by overuse and intellectual inbreeding.

Words, ennobled by time and ancient values, are among the most likely to perpetuate unrevised, wrong assumptions.

Words such as *equality* and *democracy* have become cemented in rigid walls of thought as self-sufficient pre-structured and prejudged slogans that bypass truth and common sense.

The more respectable the word, the more its application may become distorted.

It is said the Greeks invented "democracy." They met as equals in public assemblies, where elites debated elites and voted, where workers had no time to loiter, where women and slaves had no rights.

Americans too practiced democracy. They excluded women, slaves and non-landowners, both black and white.

While the word democracy and its definition remain the same, its application has changed through the years. Americans used to rely on the expertise and best judgment of their elected representatives to look after the best interests of their constituency.

Now that modern technology provides immediate communication and total coverage of information, it is possible for every individual to directly influence his government by having his opinion counted in polls of public opinion.

Now that we have a true democracy it may no longer work.

In a one-to-one vote, the mediocre citizens will always outnumber the judicious ones.

The republic of ancient Rome also enjoyed a democratic government, with a major difference. In times of war, the republic appointed a dictator for the duration of hostilities to better execute the defense of the country.

Democracy may be the best form of government for an affluent, peace-loving nation but when Hitler and other dictators precipitated World War II, Americans allowed their democratically elected president enough leeway to lead an isolationist country into the war and extended his term in office for the duration.

We Americans didn't call President Roosevelt "Dictator." Neither did the French people call President de Gaulle by that title, but for all practical purpose they both dictated their will as benevolent, wise leaders. Thus, the reality of a serious situation trumped the rigid meaning and application of a word.

The most abused terms are those provoked by social issues.
The more some people preach "tolerance" the more they convey their own intolerance of those who do not conform to their opinions.

The acceptance of other people and values by way of understanding and familiarity is not experienced as tolerance, whereas claiming to be tolerant is confirmation of controlled intolerance.

No individual should suffer the indignity of being tolerated.
No one should waste potential love just to endure what another might enjoy.

Tolerance, as a socially imposed behavior of obligatory responses is, in itself, intolerable social tyranny.

Beyond the realm of words, in the pursuit of quality in human achievements, tolerance becomes complacency that leads to creative impotence, and intolerance becomes a virtue.

Patience is another of those truisms that are accepted on face value.
Both the definition and application of the word rely on exterior observations
of human behavior. Patience is viewed as a desirable discipline for enduring
mental boredom, anguish and physical discomfort in pursuing a goal.
It is a virtue attributed to successful people and therefore worthy of
imitation.

"If Chopin could work at the piano ten hours a day, you should be able to
practice two hours!" the student is told.
Unfortunately for both student and teacher the analogy misses the point.

The difference between self-seclusion and incarceration depends on which
side of the door the key is turned.

Patience, understood as suppression of natural inclinations, is not only
unrewarding but short in duration.
No great person owes his success to this kind of patience.
Patience, as experienced by the self-motivated practitioner, is a pleasurable
excitement, intensified by a sense of purpose that overrides the lesser
sensations of tiredness, hunger and other discomforts.

What an artist calls labor of love, the uninspired observer calls patience.

There must be something better than words to clarify truth, but then, truth itself is a debatable word.

In less pretentious times "truth" was a matter of conscience or morality. A truthful person was only expected to be sincere in relating his observations or understanding of a given event or situation.

Objective truth was an attribute reserved only to God or nature. This ultimate truth that begins and ends in its self-fulfilling assertion of faith was monopolized and abused by priests, oracles and rulers.

Finally, philosophers and scientists have transferred the godly eminence of truth to its elemental component—fact. A fact is provable and, once established, is easily understood, but truth, as a unifying principle of many facts, is not the mere addition of static components.

The factual merit of a brick cannot establish the true value of a wall or a building; much less can a fact assess the true merits of a human being without the subjective evaluation of other facts in relation to specific circumstances.

Some good leaders are severely criticized for the very quality that makes them leaders because a regimented mentality finds it easier to establish a fault than judge the combined true merits of an individual.

Lawyers, psychiatrists and other experts can take opposite sides on any issue and honestly argue any portion of it as fact, though truth or justice is still entrusted to the subjective assessment of a judge or jury.

As fact,
by whatever name you know me,
that I may be:
a cheat and honest man,
a father, husband and son;
cruel, biased and kind;
ignorant, stupid and wise.
As truth,
by whatever name you call me,
you won't understand
unless you know the proportion
of all these things that I am.

"Truth, the whole truth" leading to "guilty" or "innocent" begins with human observation and concludes with humble, subjective judgment. There is a great difference between simple facts and their relative value to truth. One can have an over-abundance of facts that may never achieve truth as a judicious synthesis of relevant facts. If reason and mathematics can establish facts the collective perception of the whole mind should constitute a higher truth even if intellect cannot decipher it.

Obsession with scientific precision in ordinary situations robs the individual of confidence in his ability to recognize himself in the unproven feelings of another person. This inhibition of innate perception denies the rewards of a common truth essential to human security and meaning of life.

The subordination of higher truths to verifiable facts is analogous to the logic of the proverbial drunkard who, having lost his watch in the dark, looks for it in another place where there is more light.

There is another truth, more easily recognized than debated, deeper than reason and more inclusive than conscious judgment. It is the unifying agreement of "all the parts" that one perceives as harmony. The sense of well-being one perceives in and derives from harmony, is best achieved in the absence of explanation or discussion. Harmony is the flowing together of all the parts that give unity and meaning to our appreciation of the world and our creative efforts.

Through spontaneous sincerity the artist reveals his bias. At times he strikes a universal chord that rings true. He rearranges real materials to achieve illusions. He uses illusions to intensify reality. The more consciously he schemes the more his art fails. He may account for every known principle of composition and technical knowledge and still end up in failure.

Nothing works, short of total submission of one's effort to the brewing reservoir of assimilated experience.
Nothing adds up except the product of digested knowledge released from the rut of programmed rationality.

Truth, as an expression of responsible honesty, is seriously threatened by the misuse of the term "prejudice."

The eagerness to rectify past social injustice often inflicts a greater injustice by inhibiting honest expression of preferences and personal convictions. The word prejudice is often used slanderously to intimidate sincerity with the interjection of social-racial issues into a phenomenon rooted in the biological make-up of mankind and subject to both good and bad applications.

Prejudice also describes the non-objectionable relationship and favoritism between mother and child, husband and wife, and no less between friends. To love is to prefer someone over another. Morality itself, with all the variations in different cultures, is a benign social preference or prejudice.

A judicious person is one with preset biases to facilitate his perception of good and bad, acceptable or unacceptable.

Because a dislike is often associated with the taboo of prejudice, the spontaneous response to a dislike is usually repressed. It is this repression that either conditions neutrality or incubates that most destructive and unnecessary emotion—hate.

Bias is a word and the word is biased.

One calls you loyal, the other calls you biased.
To one you are strong-minded, to the other stubborn.
Thus one knows his friends through expressed bias—one of which is love.

The student rebellion of the sixties against sterile intellectualism in higher education degenerated into a free-for-all of side issues that still persists decades later—victims identifying other victims of all denominations, races, and physical descriptions. Claims of injustice toward African Americans, women and other minorities produce more claims of injustice than ideas for remedies.

The student-discontents of the sixties became the teacher-discontents of the nineties, with no better understanding of the fundamental causes of the original revolt.
At universities and colleges, racism and sexism have become mere root-words in a field of growing "isms" that reduce common conversation to a skill of evasive side-stepping in a mine field of verbal taboos.

Under the heading of discrimination, injustice is claimed against race, nationality and gender, as well as occupation, social status, age, handicap and physical appearance.

Most expressions of honest judgment and taste tread on the brink of social disaster, for fear of stepping on a trigger-word that, like a booby trap, is wired to any subject and innocent reference that might offend the "abused."

Since most teachers are also victims of their own education, "The blind leading the blind" comes to mind, but who would dare call a blind person "blind?" "Political Correctness" or more correctly—legitimate hypocrisy—would have us call a disabled person "physically challenged" or "differently abled."

The verbal camouflage offends truth and brings ridicule to a sober reality. Many great people excelled because they compensated for some personal disadvantage. Homer was blind and Demosthenes stuttered. Michelangelo was ugly. Leonardo D'Vinci was a homosexual in an intolerant society. Caesar was epileptic and Napoleon was short. Beethoven was deaf and Roosevelt was crippled. Stephen Hawking can neither speak nor move. None of these people suggested that the world should level its hills and mountains so that they might be spared the climbing.

By removing obstacles, society removes the vital impetus of compensation for one's own limitations. Success or satisfaction in life depends on personal initiative and choice to enjoy a slower rhythm of life or take pride in prevailing over one's own misfortune.

Society's obsession with equality overcompensates for the handicapped and fails to challenge the able-bodied so that all can keep in step with the average.

Equality is the most emotionally loaded, inflammatory word that ever inspired political and social causes. Any challenge to the concept of equality evokes more mob psychology than reason. Nevertheless, in a world of matter and living things equality is a rare occurrence. Neither history nor current knowledge demonstrates that equality ever characterized humanity or that it would contribute to the betterment of society and individuals.

This statement should not be confused with the principle of equal opportunity—that no person should be impeded from developing to the best of his or her potential. The right to equal opportunity, however, does not imply that two individuals have equal sensitivity for recognizing an opportunity or have equal motivation to seize it.

Equality as a human phenomenon is a myth. As myth may serve the expression of human aspirations, so equality may serve a rebel's cry as he climbs the social ladder to improve his lot in life. In spite of all the historical changes and improvements that have shifted groups and individuals up and down the socioeconomic structure the structure itself never changed.

Sociologists may make factual statements on the inequality of material possessions, but until they learn to take the pulse of individual happiness they will not know the "haves" from the "have-nots."

As truly as
democracy is rule by majority,
humanity is a large-bodied creature
with a head that leads   *and a tail that follows.*

As long as individuals are born with different capacities of body and mind they will contribute to society different skills at different levels of performance.

If the whole of society were to be lifted to the optimum level of individual potential, there would be the same relative differences between groups and between individuals.

Even in democratic societies with the professed aim of equality, the "ideal" is in sharp contrast to reality. The standard curve of social distribution would reveal the inevitable pattern: a majority of people in the middle, a privileged few on one end, and an underprivileged minority on the other.

The fact that social inequalities have endured and still persist poses the question: Is it social injustice or is it an unavoidable condition for survival and the advancement of mankind? Evidence suggests that humanity prospered not in spite of but because of individual and group differences.

A degree of discontent is a necessary dynamic of life and a prerequisite to the experience of self-fulfillment. The perennial social struggle may well be the vital element that energizes society with creative spirit, humane values and noble deeds.

The above statements do not consider how different social systems address the disparity between rich and poor; how to provide a buffer against misery, poverty and handicaps in a compassionate society. They merely point out the raw nature of nature.

Equality has become a slogan that confuses individual equity with regimented sameness.

All schools profess educational equality and yet they rely on discriminating grades to identify the best, the good and the average student.
Those people who cry "foul" in questioning the validity of tests on the basis of gender or cultural differences are confirming the fact that people are individuals and can only achieve equity through differentiated treatment. Goals that set false expectations can make a normal person feel insufficient.

In art classes the teacher must confront each student at whatever level of development the individual may be. One's cultural background and all that contributes to personal differences are unavoidable points of departure for teaching a medium of self-expression that usually leads to self-understanding and, sometimes, art.

In creative activities there can be as many valid answers as there are students in class. Once honesty of expression is established, the work is ranked on the basis of technical proficiency, richness and scope of artistic concept.
Thus, equality is achieved by using discriminating patterns of teaching to meet the needs and aptitude of each individual.

There is something reassuring about a word associated with popular causes, as there is security in measurements and symmetrical numbers, especially when values are in doubt.

The social experiment with the 50/50 proposition, to achieve equality between husband and wife, is an insensitive oversimplification of a basic human relationship.
If a mathematical equation must be applied to marriage it should read 100% of each spouse and let the quality of harmony between them determine balance.
Husband and wife need not have matched energy and talents.

It is the very complementary qualities in men and women that make marriage functional and desirable. It is the difference between children and parents that makes their relationship essential and mutually rewarding.
It is their mutual respect and love that makes each of them equal in all their differences.

It is when a child grows up to the comparable strength and maturity of his parents that separation becomes natural and advisable to avoid the consequences of sharing a home with equals.

One learns that two positive poles of a magnet repel each other, and two positive wires burn the fuse; that artistic compositions require a dominant theme to achieve unity and meaning, and that repetition of equal shapes without a dominant image is mere decoration; that every story has a dominant character and every stage has a star; that groups of peers elect a leader to facilitate procedures and unify efforts; that animals group under a dominant male or a dominant female, and that seldom are there two rulers on a throne.

Evidence suggests it is not equality but the principle of subordination that characterizes life and creation, whether it is subordination of animals to plants or fellow humans to the sun, the universe or God.

Subordination between two individuals may be temporary or reciprocal.
It may be a condition of love or need for belonging and security.
It may be a commitment to a noble cause or the pursuit of individual betterment in relation to a higher standard than one's own.

The negative definition of subordination, already loaded with social bias, is made more offensive by the juxtaposition of its meaning with that of equality.

Thus, a word teams up with another word, gaining social impact and special meaning, independent of its broader context and actual application to life. Thus, a word is directed to an ego already conditioned to respond to symbols more than substance.

As a mechanism in the order of creation, subordination and domination are opposite views of the same structure. The difference exists in the consciousness of man, in the way he relates to a universe that expands away from him and within himself—toward the larger and the smaller dimensions of creation. From this middle point, man chooses to be a working part of something big or to dominate a lesser thing. He usually chooses both, but it is the first option that provides the greater dynamics of life and best describes mankind.

What great achievement was ever recorded that didn't require one's total submission of energy and talent?
What simple task was ever performed that didn't require adaptation of tools and skills to the intent of the project at hand?

Even an honest question implies subordination, in the willingness to hear another's opinion and in conceding one's ignorance.
The very experience of beauty is submission to the compelling mood of an object, a person or landscape.
Love, adventure, loyalty and courage all require the subordination of a self-centered ego to a greater dimension of life.
A parent and child are locked in a relationship of mutual subordination.
The child is helpless without the parent and the parent is helplessly addicted to fulfilling the child's every need.
One climbs a mountain to be part of something bigger than oneself.

All one learns from life is resubmitted to life.
Whatever one masters is discarded in the back chambers of the mind,
as one discards a toy that has been outgrown.
It is the next problem, the next adventure that captivates one's interest
rather than what has already been mastered.

The concept of dominance or control as implied in the word "master," denoting a person of superior creative talent, does not contradict the principle of subordination. In spite of mastery over skills, an artist's every attempt to create must begin with an unknown. The creative process is a humble blending of undefined urges and hopes in the search for something that does not yet exist.

Even Beethoven's apparent arrogance was the manifestation of a possessed man. He was possessed and controlled by the same uncompromising passion that dictated his music—a music that was nurtured by a persistent fear of failure and humiliation over his loss of hearing. When this great artist contemplated quitting his tormenting career and realized that he didn't have a choice but to obey the deeper urging of his soul, his music achieved a greater dimension. The sure mastery of form that characterizes his Fifth Symphony expanded into a more submissive abandon in his later works and reached beyond the confines of conscious control.

Concentration, in a serious undertaking, is often achieved through a deliberate, self-induced hypnosis that begins as simple contemplation and may culminate in a deep trance. This process of expanding the mind's horizon awakens dormant sensations that combine to engulf the ego as an integral part of a timeless reassembling of old experiences and new responses.

When an artist emerges from his deep concentration and achieves psychological distance from a successful work, he views his art as if for the first time. The pride he may feel regarding the finished product is usually a manifestation of his humble realization that his art is surprisingly superior to any attribute of his conscious self.

The concept of subordination is just as valid when presented from the point of view of willed control.

A General channels his orders through a chain of subordinates, who, in turn, give orders to lower subordinates all the way down to the essential unit—the foot-soldier.

So moves a functional army. So operates a successful business. So a thinker organizes his ideas. So an artist organizes all elements of his composition. Even rearranging furniture is a process of subordinating the pieces to the size, shape and decor of the room.

Ecology is a concept of total subordination of all life and earthly components to the organic unity of the world.

A

Word	may convey a limited meaning, but,
Meaning	is not punctuated word by word.
Hunger	is not an undesirable experience. It is
Appetite	a condition of health, a prerequisite to pleasure and survival.
Pain	is not punishment. It is a compelling signal to spare the body from damage.
Pleasure	uses the same nerve that feels pain.
	To remove the nerve of pain is to remove pleasure.

Too hot or too cold, as all the variations of good and bad, are perceptions of mere proportions of potential good.

Blotches of colors and scribbles animate good paintings.

Sound may lead to noise or music.

From a given piano one hears good melodies and bad tunes.

From the same keyboard each soul may structure harmony out of discord.

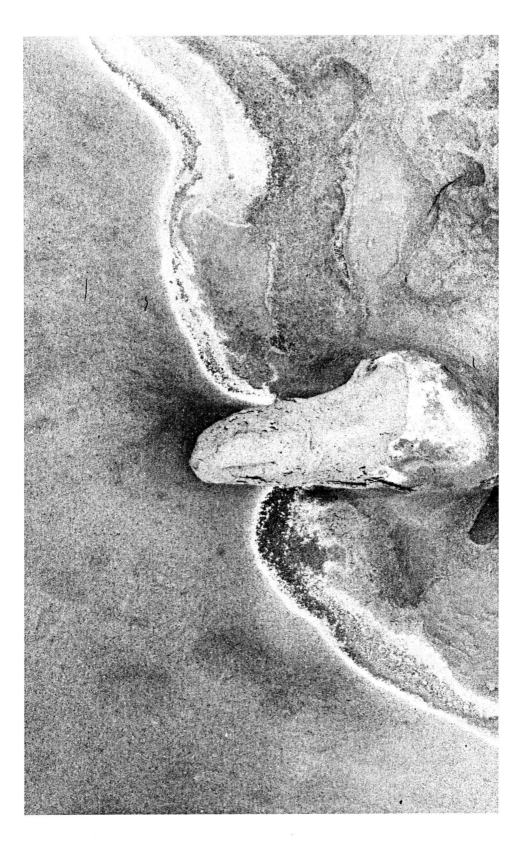

Thought and Feeling

I feel, "therefore I am."
I am, before I think.
I think to expand and protect what I am.

Were that we were so simple as not to know where the mind resides
And responded to the world with insightful gut-feelings
We could then accept our body as the abode of a godly spirit
To fill the hollows of ignorance with warm assurance
That, even as we sleep and dream unresolved dreams
A benign intelligence regulates the flow of life
And swells our breasts with calm confirmation
With each sigh and heartbeat.

Were that we were so bold
As to let the child in us prevail
And let our innocence regain Eden.
We could then outflank doubt
By exclaiming "Wow!" before asking "Why?"
To let our senses pasture on green discoveries
To energize life and creative thinking
To flavor knowledge with felt meaning.

Because I am, I feel. Because I feel, I have cause to think. These two aspects of the mind take turns in prevailing like twins playing leapfrog.

There is no real need to separate reason from sense perception just to identify what role each plays. However, thinking thrives on words and words have a way of taking things apart. As such, I must identify which part of the mind is the vehicle and which is content.

The way the game is played within my skull leaves no doubt as to which is mechanics and which is substance. There, thinking and feelings are usually a team, though, when reason tries to play alone, ideas wilt before they are formed. Even when feeling and reason climax together the joy of success stays while reason recedes in the mind's limbo to await the next urging of a perceived problem or an invitation to share in a creative venture.

As we travel the webbed ways of the mind, it seems clear that reason is a conveyance while feeling is both fuel and substance.

Feeling is the cause and consequence of every expression.
It is the cause and consequence of every response.
Feeling is the shapeless ghost orbiting the mind in search of a vent of expression to give it a tangible form to make it transferable to another soul.

The dimension of feeling is not independent of intellect.
Feeling is the reward for what a person does well.
It is the negative consequence for what a person does wrong.
No human activity achieves satisfaction without the agreement of feeling.
No long-term project can be endured without that felt determination, too
often dismissed as motivation, as if it were not a functional part of the mind.

Thinking, as a problem-solving mechanical process, is a mere pause in the
harmony of living between a point of imbalance and recovery.
Thinking, per se, results from doubt or ignorance or unresolved problems.

Intellectual investigation, or reasoning, must connect with human relevance
to translate information into a working and ever-present understanding.
What a person is actively thinking is too raw for expressive purposes and too
immature a basis for judgment.

Working knowledge is the integrated fluid experience that saturates the
mind beyond specific recall. It is that forgotten knowledge that reemerges
intuitively as immediate response in moments of danger or contributes depth
of the whole mind in creative endeavors.

Thinking is too static a method for understanding the living spirit that characterizes man and his dynamic perception of the world.

The very utterance of what a person knows creates a new reality.
Several people describing the same sunset may all agree on what they see, but, if each person were to express his personal experience it would result in different realities, or different emphases, usually viewed as distortions of a fixed phenomena.

Two individuals have no trouble identifying and agreeing on the shape of an object in its true proportions, but when an artist animates it with his personal vitality, the resulting distortion is for expressive purposes and the expressed message becomes reality, not the neutral object.

A song is not a distortion of the spoken word. It is the superimposition of music upon language to convey a greater experience beyond the limits of words. This complex reorientation of sound and time is perceived and appreciated instantaneously by our senses.

Given that all we understand from reasoning and all we know from direct experience modify every new perception, it follows that what we perceive through our senses is the core and the whole of human reality.

To be is to respond with personal awareness to ideas, moods and physical forces.

One brings no meaning to the concept of objective truth without conceding that all experiences and human insights originate with our senses.

Speculation and abstract conclusions about phenomena beyond the reach of our senses are only extensions and creative applications of principles previously learned from direct experience. Though we may devise criteria of objective standards for assessing human achievement, creative output is always personal and emotionally driven.

Most human expressions are self-serving, honest responses to our inner urge to achieve meaningful communication with fellow man and spiritual communion with all of creation. A person can only control the integrity of his own thoughts and expressions.

One cannot count on the spontaneous responses of other people, but, at times, when we achieve sufficient harmony and depth of expression, we also touch the universal nerve that binds humanity in appreciation of our collective spiritual nature.

No thought or deed can produce or impart a felt-meaning if it is not born of sincere concern or shared excitement.

Honesty in art is not a conscious virtue. It isn't even a choice.
Nothing important is ever produced if the creative process does not feed back the spiritual energy one puts into it.

In a materialist society, commercial and public institutions may indulge in deception or hypocrisy, but false responses or pretended feelings on a personal level is more than deceit. It is self denial.

Honesty of expression and response is the qualifier of all the other principles of life, including goodness and truth.
As one matures, he may modify his conclusions and make different choices, but sincerity remains a constant virtue throughout one's life and in all human relationships.

One should not be intimidated by prevailing tastes in expressing his preferences!

One does not achieve clear vision by looking directly at the sun.
It is reflected light that reveals the shapes and colors of worldly realities.

Our intuitive appreciation of the world, with love and empathy for life, our response to fellowman's ideas and expressions, and our creative output, fully account for what we understand about ourselves.

Looking directly into the working contents of one's own mind through the narrow view of reason is like pressing one's nose up against a Seurat painting to study its content one dot at a time.

Not unlike riding a bicycle, the more one looks too closely at the pedals the more the road becomes an unfocused blur. The more one views the broader vista ahead, the steadier the ride and more wholesome the experience.

Seeking understanding through a strictly rational process, independent of felt insights, can only condition one's mind to a limited use of its vast potentials.

Meditation, or the period of incubation preceding most ideas, is an experience of relaxed freedom from the conditioned ruts of reason. The limbering up of our central nervous system allows intuition and sense perception to kick-in, broadening our horizon and bringing the whole mind into play.

Thought cannot achieve meaningful depths without the emotional rewards that sustain our endless efforts to promote and protect our quality of life. More important than the intellectual programming of the mind is the use and enjoyment of what a person has already accumulated and digested.

Thinking, as a problem-solver, is of transitory value.
The process of learning to ride a bike is what one strives to get beyond to enjoy the benefit of having learned.

What we really know and enjoy is what we no longer think about. While thought and trial and error are essential to learning skills, our spontaneous response to the world makes use of all that we already know. What we know sharpens our perception and makes our response a more inclusive experience.

Once we are free from thinking about the mechanics of riding a bike the mind surrenders its inhibition and all that surrounds us becomes a concentrated experience.
We enjoy the confirmation of our body through the straining of our legs, the sound of the wheels on the road and the caress of the wind on our face as we become one with the dynamics of life.

The mental discipline of abstracting precise facts and measurements from the reality of human experience should be a conscious effort for meeting special needs, not a chronic condition that makes of the mind more a tool than the recipient of enriched experience.

Thought may be an enjoyable creative experience in itself that might eventually contribute greater appreciation to one's intuitive responses, but at moments of deep contemplation or spiritual fulfillment, reason and explanations are totally disruptive.

There is a great difference between making love and explaining the process. Love in its simple acceptance as a fulfilling experience is much better than having it analyzed and intellectually dismembered as a selfish act.
Yes, a mother loves her child because she loves to love him.
This kind of selfishness applies to every benevolent act and ethical behavior of a good person who does everything to satisfy his own craving for love.
It is hoped that this kind of reasoning evaporates in the heat of passion, so that a human being can regain some of the uninhibited abandon in felt responses enjoyed by most other creatures.

A spontaneous insight can be supplemented with the slower process of reason but reason should not substitute or inhibit this direct and personal way of knowing.

Self-detachment as a means of achieving unbiased rational goals is a farce. The pursuit of impersonal truth is often propelled by a desire for abstract order that may reach the intensity of passion. But, it is one thing to achieve balanced emotions and another to deny one's emotions in a purposeful deed or thought.

The "cool" athlete is emotionally driven and steadied by his concentrated sense of purpose. The apparent neutrality of an artist toward a nude model is not a lack of sexual response but rather the added sensuousness he derives from his own work that results in a balanced, professional concentration.

The rigid methodology of the scientific process is often the exterior appearance of a creative adventure that culminates in personal satisfaction and a sense of beauty.

It is the emulation of this exterior rigidity, without the supporting motivation of purpose and pleasure, that plagues education with indifference in the process of learning.

Teasing the mind out of complacency and restoring balance to the human organism is a full time occupation.

If hunger didn't compel people to hunt or farm there would be little purpose and sense of accomplishment in their lives.

If people didn't need protection from the elements they would not build homes, make clothes, or seek security and social experience in organized society.

One knows comfort as relief from discomfort.

One pursues excitement as relief from boredom.

For every extreme, one finds pleasure in taking a counter measure.

It is no wonder that in climates with contrasting seasons people are most active and resourceful. Where seasons are variable, individuals and families experience the full range of seasonal moods and sentiments. They are relaxed and carefree in summer but become solicitous and caring in the fall. Nothing warms the heart and pulls families together more than the common threat of a cold winter.

Few things compare with the intimate experience of winter nesting with loved ones. When spring arrives, few souls are more appreciative than those who have known the solitude of winter.

A bit of adversity is necessary to meaningful living. A person needs to experience tiredness to enjoy rest and needs to be rested to enjoy getting tired. Hunger is anticipation of enjoying a meal, just as uneasiness is only the beginning of a creative response that rewards the soul all the way to the next challenge.

Being spoiled is lack of appreciative response, associated with people who have been unduly protected from hurt and disappointment, thus lacking the "bad" as a basis for keener appreciation of the "good." The worst of pain and suffering can be a measure of complementary pleasures when pain becomes motivation for restructuring itself at a higher level of spiritual renewal.

Nothing worth doing can be void of feelings. Even the unemotional calm of a surgeon is, in fact, a heightened sense of feeling, brought in balance by an equal sense of purpose in his effort to save a life.

Feeling is the mental energy that calmly sustains the process of thought and human activity. It is the frustration of unresolved problems that heightens the ultimate satisfaction with their solution. It takes emotional energy to establish in the mind the forward momentum of self-discovery.

All we know as feeling, and all the skills we learn to evoke and enhance feeling, is the essence of human experience.

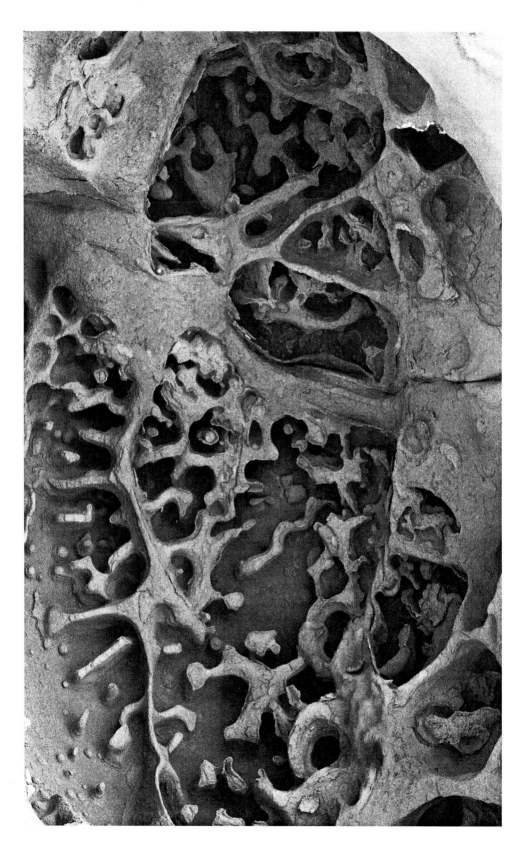

The Influence of Science on Understanding

So much of life is made idle as spirit and matter are analyzed, separated and left lying.

Analytical, objective thinking did not begin with the onset of modern science. From Plato to Descartes philosophers have labored with the idea of pure thinking. Though beauty and the sensuous have always been an integral part of human experience, they sought the essence of truth solely in what verbal logic could explain.

Thinking for its own sake, oblivious to felt responses, became thinking without content and eventually resulted in Descartes' play of words, "I think therefore I am."

Though scientists use the same discipline of impersonal objectivity, they also use intuitive insights and practical tests as inventors or artists. Both in the studio and in the lab one uses the word "beautiful!" to express success.

Formal education adopted the impersonal methodology of science as the discipline for most areas of study.
This special discipline, best suited for exploring the physical world, is displacing educational efforts to cultivate human values that make the enrichment of a sensitive mind the true measure of human development.

It is far better to live by a philosophy than be a scholar of many…
For without a philosophy the mind has nothing with which to engage new ideas.

Though knowledge cannot be assimilated into anything more elevated and more useful than personal judgment, both teachers and students apologize whenever they express a personal opinion that might distort objective truth. What good is an education that does not contribute to personal value or opinion?

This mental state of neutral "open-mindedness" is underscored by doubts on priorities, direction and purpose of life.
A young person who is unsure and confused because he lacks a unifying purpose in life invariably ends up taking a course in psychology.

The universal appeal of a course dealing with the mind is reinforced by the prevailing reliance on dissected bits of truth to resolve organic problems.
To a person already lacking meaningful cohesion of the idle facts crowding his mind, an introduction to psychology does anything but restore the unity of a feeling intelligence.

At best, the course takes the mind apart to show how the pieces break down into even smaller pieces, to further fragment a mind already lacking the impetus of self-confidence to put the pieces back together.
I know, because so many of my students confessed having found in their creative work a sense of well-being and unity of mind they had sought in their study of the mind.

From early childhood, formal education strives to retrain the mind to suspect and eventually discount all unreasoned perceptions.

This practice condemns all but the strongest to a lifetime of rehashing insipid, secondhand information.

It denies understanding the spontaneous sustenance of the senses.

It denies the human ego the security of immediate and continuous judgment.

Though creative scientists, political innovators, artists and practical inventors are familiar with the phenomena of sudden insight, the word "intuition" is still suspect among some academics who believe that valid ideas arise strictly from systematic, rational efforts.

Intuitive understanding is usually attributed to children before they learn the virtue of doubt. It is also attributed to all creative people.

The scientist proceeds from his tentative hypothesis to formulate a principle by which to explain the mechanics of the physical world.

The artist too obeys his insightful impulses to give form and vitality to abstract ideas.

Intuition is the deeply informed judgment beyond conscious recall.

It is that quality of the mind that requires and sustains self-confidence.

It is the love-child of empathy—the intimate rapport between creator and his medium of expression. It is that quality of mental unity that becomes disrupted through doubt and fear—fear to make choices, fear to be.

Intuition is the child in every person that either hides or rides his fantasies.

The more secure the man, the more the child in him is free to play.

Most innovative ideas reflect a break from an established pattern of thinking. Albert Einstein was not a good student of mathematics and Frank Lloyd Wright was not a good student of architectural engineering. They were innovators of different patterns of thought. The creative urge to explore, beyond the parameters of general consensus, is a basic ingredient of being human.

Life is a continuous process of personal discoveries with arbitrary goals that mark not the end but new beginnings. Quality of life relates to our quality of experience in the process of daily living, not the momentary pause of reaching a goal.

Most scientists and other creative thinkers agree that it is more fun to discover knowledge than to have it, much as everyone else agrees that it is more enjoyable to satisfy an appetite than to be satiated.

This basic principle, which regulates the creative mind or intelligence, is usually lost in the mechanics of formal education. Most teachers are trained to be custodians rather than producers of knowledge, and schools are geared for the simple task of transmitting information and skills. Thus, education begins with a finished product or formula and backtracks through its inanimate, factual components.

This replaying of knowledge in reverse sequence inhibits creativity and robs one's mind of the ultimate joy of personal discovery.

The way I understand it:
The mind functions like the hands of a clock.
An idea or a sudden insight rings at twelve.
Once an insight is submitted to the rational process, the hand begins
a new count. Twelve becomes zero, the point of departure.
Few minds are wound enough to go past the midway point and complete
the upward sweep of reason back to the original insight.
When lacking skill or scope, the mind stalls short of twelve.
The glimpse of truth fails to reconstruct itself and may never ring again
as intuitive insight or proven fact.

In other words, there are three phases of understanding:

- First is the self-sufficient, intuitive perception that may lead to

- the intellectual process of resubmitting the spontaneous insight to
  the long circuit of critical analysis that may lead back to

- the point of departure, with proof of what the mind had
  already understood, to begin anew with an enriched intuitive
  perception.

The fulfilling rewards of the mind are those experienced at the basic level
of innocent intuition or at the higher level where rational understanding
becomes an integral part of intuitive perception.
The middle phase of understanding—the intellectual phase—is only a
transition between two levels of integrated knowledge. The intellectual
phase, though important, is hardly the coming together of the whole mind.

Some truths are more direct and simpler than their explanation. Analytical appreciation may follow the aesthetic experience of hearing a symphony but the intellectual after-play is hardly the cause of such an experience. There is no substitute for seeing art and hearing music as a means to spiritual fulfillment and practical conditioning of human sensitivity.

Science's successful use of analysis as a method of research has added vigor to the academic tradition of explaining everything, including aesthetic theories that never crossed an artist's mind.

Analyzing an aesthetic experience is like plucking a flower, one petal at a time, to explain the beauty that is being destroyed.

At all levels of development, judgment is the relative summation of what a person understands. It is a true expression of one's basic values. The learned tendency to analyze and reduce the working unity of our mind into separate components undoes the synthesis of assimilated knowledge.

Not trusting one's own judgment is comparable to spending a lifetime programming a computer and then failing to use the compiled data just because the rational mind cannot trust the automatic output of accumulated knowledge.

Rapid information is for computers!
Communication between souls should linger long enough to become communion.

The computer offers tangible evidence of which component of the mind is peripheral and which is central to human consciousness, what function of the brain is transferable to a mechanical device and what is exclusively basic to the human mind.

Creativity is an obvious function restricted to human intelligence, as is the capacity for contemplating those beautiful and spiritual experiences that give substance to meaning and scope to life.

The convenience of a computer performing mechanical tasks, rapidly and precisely, should have freed mankind for more creative and fulfilling experiences. Instead, the delegation of this function of the mind to a computer has further obsessed society with the single dimension of speed. The better things in life have their own rhythm, and like music, must be played to the beat of the human heart.

The merits and limitations of a computer make obvious an important inconsistency in our concept of knowledge, how we gain it and how we evaluate it.

A computer retains data and reliably recalls it, promptly and unchanged, but, any material a person learns is qualified by what he already knows and acquires a different dimension in different individuals.
The mere recalling of information makes available the original raw data, out of context with its present value in the organic unity of an individual mind.

The Aesthetic and the Spiritual

The **aesthetic** *and the* **spiritual** *experiences
are contained in one another.*

In world-oriented "primitive religions" the spirit resided in the ceremonial masks and totems. The object of beauty was the objectified spirit. Through colors and forms, songs and dances, art was the language of the gods. Heaven was the best of this world.

Throughout history, mankind found security and spiritual fulfillment in art and religion.
Both are expressions of man's intuitive inner being that transcends understanding of the physical realities of the world.
Both celebrate the gift of life to evoke a sense of the sacred and give meaning to the pleasures and adversities of daily living.

Early man, in his insightful, simple celebrations of nature, may have achieved the full depth of religious experience.

As man addressed the gods his words became songs.
Dance, to the beat of hollow logs, echoed the rhythm of the human heart.
All that filled the senses was confirmation of life and the human spirit.
Rituals were self-fulfilling expressions and required no explanation.
The aesthetic-spiritual experience was the religious experience.
It gave total insight into the harmonious oneness of man, nature and God.

The spiritual-aesthetic experience is the most humanizing and binding relationship between individuals and the whole of mankind.

In no other dimension of life are we more homogeneous and trusting of one another than in the shared pursuit of beauty and spiritual harmony. Even when countries are at war with each other, people will continue to read the literature and listen to the music of the enemy. Our spiritual affinity with fellow humans is the common bond that extends to a broader connection with other creatures and nature.

It is this perception of physical belonging to something greater than oneself that promotes the sense of security, known as faith or trust, in a higher dimension of infinite power.

Religious devotees have knelt before holy paintings and sculptures, the concentrated vision of artists who achieved nothing more than worldly beauty. When Michelangelo had filled the ceiling of the Sistine Chapel with God and his naked creation, it was His Holiness who prayed before the artisan's vision.

The spirit cannot take substance from an unknown heaven, and priests can only dispense as much spirit as a worldly mind can assemble.

No religious authority can add or take away from the best of artistic expressions. Religious music does not take meaning from religion.

It is religion that utilizes the musical experience to give spiritual substance to the philosophical concept of God and religion.

Though only some music is designated "sacred," Beethoven's "Ode to Joy" rises independently to heaven, as does the voice of any soul who sings the glory of life.

Of all human attempts to reach God, in sacred rituals and in the darkest moments of our lives, music has the greatest reach toward the unknown and into our souls.

Like God, it is pure abstraction, real and indescribable.
It has many forms and moods and none can be isolated or combined into anything recognizable, as animal or landscape.

The spiritual experience, like music, is the felt perception of what is beyond our capacity to identify or explain. Like music, it speaks directly to our soul and leaves us fulfilled with a reality that invites no intrusion, only contentment.

Like God, we give music a name and a face to render it visible, but we become annoyed when a musicologist trivializes it with an explanation as if a sublime experience requires rational validation.

The visual arts also contribute their spiritual vitality to religious structures and rites, but, because visual arts also represent and illustrate, the aesthetic component is not as easily isolated for clear-cut analogies with pure spirit.

We create art and invent a beautiful Heaven to project our soul beyond our world and lifespan, but even as we speak of faith and the unknown, we blunt the edges of reality to keep our deepest concerns at intellectual distance.

Heaven, hell, eternity: these are some of the concepts we shove out of reach in the limbo of the future.

If our thoughts could accept the real implication of eternity it would register in the mind not in future tense but as something that has always been and from which we have emerged as a continuous process of life.

If, in viewing the future, we would also look in the rear-view mirror, we would see that the road ahead is the same road we leave behind and inevitably conclude that eternity is now, and now is the only reality we know.

Amid growing things
Just before sundown,
"How old are you?" asked my son.
I worked the hoe to the end of a furrow
Before answering, "Forty-four."
The child followed with measured steps;
One foot spaced the seed,
The other pressed it down.
"Years are too long for me to understand!
Tell me, how many days since you were born?"
Down on my knees I granulated the ground;
Patted it smooth with both hands and
Let a finger plow for the answer
Hidden just under my skin.
"Here it is!"—A life counted in days –
Written on the soil that will reclaim it.
He looked at numbers and I at sunset.
"Now I know!" said my flesh.

The concept God has evoked symbols ranging from celestial bodies to animal and human forms, all of which have a reasonable basis. If God is everything it must be present in any given thing.

Pagan religions had numerous gods and goddesses each embodying a special function. The god of war, beauty, fertility and on to the last identifiable human concern made God an approachable entity.

The monotheistic concept of God recognizes the principle of organic unity, or singularity, as a necessary quality of a Supreme entity. But even this concept of God was broken down into three separate entities including human incarnation.

To complete a full cycle, God was again made more approachable by adding, as intermediaries, a multitude of saints, each a patron of a significant aspect of life.

Inspired wisdom conceived a multi-dimensional deity—the Trinity—that in my mundane understanding signifies:

> The principle of order and unity;
> The materialization of energy into tangible forms,
> The spiritual-aesthetic experience of life's energy.

To evoke from the material the spirit,
To translate the spirit into material forms,
To appreciate and be a creative participant in life is to be one with God.

From where I stand,
faith carries more truth than a half-spun thought
and weighs much less than fear of death.
Sorrow or compassion is evidence of life.
The deceased does not suffer from his own passing.
If eternal I am, I must have died many times
as a consequence of having lived.
My proof of eternal resurrection is my last arrival.

When Galileo insisted "*eppur si muove*," science challenged the Church as an equal adversary, and prevailed.
What science prevailed over was an old-fashioned notion of truth—a self-limiting concept of God that could not free itself from the trappings of "sacred words."

In simpler times one might have preferred the durability of an innocent dogma to a revision of faith. But, having fed on the forbidden Tree of Knowledge, mankind is finding it difficult to reconcile present enlightenment with old conclusions of a limited creator of a small segment of an immense universe.

At the same time, we sense the lack of another reality that reason does not account for. As we sing or play, as we dance or make music together or explore the woods to view unspoiled nature and listen to the sounds of fellow creatures, we know the reality of human spirit as a culminating experience.

After millennia of trying, it seems obvious that philosophers have been pursuing "truth" or God on a circular path that provides intellectual exercise or so called "enlightenment" without a point of arrival.
While science is still exploring the elusive principle of a basic law of nature from a runaway universe, mankind finds God a reassuring concept in view of our relative ignorance of the scope and immensity of creation.

The Judeo-Christian Bible is part history and part inspired writing.
It is a record of much of the best ideals and practical understanding of its time. Besides the symbolic rendition of the genesis of man, besides the basic commandments that still define our ethical conduct, it includes down-to-earth concerns for practical, everyday living. The wisdom and visions of prophets and philosophers, kings, writers, and scholars of the day, were the collective voice of God that taught moral laws, personal hygiene and mental health; set taboos on food and vices that might corrupt the body and human spirit.

The inspired ideals and the observed ways of nature became the laws of God. Religious tenets furnished the big umbrella that encompassed all the current knowledge of this world, limited as it might have been then.
Once the laws of God became incised on stone and copper scrolls, the words became sacred and unalterable, even after humanity had gained a better understanding of the greater immensity of God's creation.

The universality of spiritual experience as conveyed in all religions and aesthetic expressions is confirmation of a dimension of life than enriches and supersedes all material realities.

What does it matter whether the Bible is script or scripture, or whether Eden may have been a place somewhere in time or a poetic rendition of a basic ideal.
Truth is not limited to material facts and God cannot be contained in a verbal cage.

Because of current understanding, we humans have reasons to be humble as worldwide communication shrinks our world and we perceive ourselves as a small family hanging on to a half-lit fragment of a primordial explosion in the abyss of an infinite unknown.

Unless we expand our spiritual concept of God to encompass and put in proper perspective all dimensions of creation, we may lose the unity of matter and spirit, without which there is no meaning to God or man.

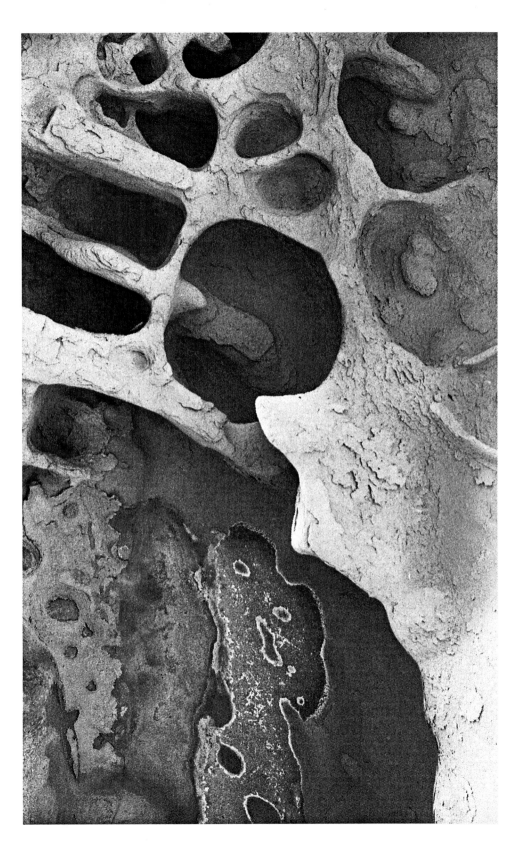

Life Is Response

Life is response to life.
Meaning is a quality of human response.

No pledge of verbal reassurance is as convincing
as the reality of the senses—the meeting of eyes,
the clasping of hands, the mutual pressure of two bodies.

From the moment a human being is born, he screams his displeasure at losing the security of the womb.

He begins life with an irresistible expression of want, with a love-provoking cry of helplessness that prompts the strong to protect the young, that sets the pattern of continued dependence on fellow humans, for comfort and approval, for health and survival.

Responding to basic drives beyond reason and choice, the newborn accepts the nipple of sustenance and milks its contents while holding the whole world in his hands.

His first cry is both response and expression of his being alive.

His first delight is the touch of reunited flesh, pressed gently by loving arms. Even before his eyes can focus he reaches out with possessive hands to grasp onto anything within reach, to let touch confirm his claim to life.

All that an infant sees he wants to touch. All that he touches he brings to his mouth to explore the taste and smell of things.

A newborn responds to music and motion. He responds to the sound of his toy banging on his crib as he explores a rhythm of his own making. His appreciative response to the world is a true indication of his spiritual capacity.

Few simple delights are more pure and fulfilling than a child's rolling downhill on a grassy slope, filling his nostrils near the roots of life and coming to rest, facing the sky, to let his thoughts soar with the passing clouds.

"Look, but do not touch!" are the inhibiting words that most parents use to admonish young children, forgetting that human senses like to feel in unison.
It is natural to supplement vision with touch, taste and smell.
It is normal to caress a beautiful shape with the fingers of our vision.
It is convenient to have eyes at the tips of our fingers as they scan our pockets for car keys or give vision to a tender touch in the dark.

Inhibition of one's responses is, at times, a necessary restraint in exercising discretion and good will toward others.
Caution, as a natural response to the unfamiliar, is another inhibition that partially explains biased responses. A child exhibits limited preferences until understanding and familiarity pushes the limits of personal relationship toward a more inclusive recognition of fellow-people, beyond family and friends.

The expression of one's preferences, at any stage of personal development, will unavoidably entail discriminating choices, not necessarily wise or just but essential to the exercising of judgment and meaningful living.

It is in our likes and dislikes that we most honestly acknowledge what we are and signal to others our common bonds as fellow human-beings and as distinct individuals.

Confidence in our ability to evoke positive responses is based on our realization that we are more alike than we are different.
We share an innate sense of order, common needs and aspirations.
We communicate with each other on the assumption of having matched feelings and the ability to recognize ourselves in one another.
Recognition of traits that make us alike is essential to our security and comfort.

It is this reassurance of belonging to the family of man that gives us confidence to respond and reveal our innermost personal bias in artistic expressions and choice of friends.

One's preference or taste is a discriminating response of all our senses.
It is the oldest and most basic perception of the mind.
Primordial man met his vital needs by discerning the right smell and taste of food, by recognizing visual patterns and the feel of things.
Through selective appetites man discriminated between right and wrong on the basis of tastes conducive to health and well being.

One knows what he knows, by whatever means he has learned it,
even if he doesn't understand the mechanics of what he knows.
One knows that fire is hot without understanding what causes heat.
One may judge that a soup is good without knowing its recipe.
Knowing a soup's ingredients has its own value, but without the experience
of taste it is unlikely that a person would care to pursue the why, where and
how of a soup.
Taste is responsive knowledge.
Taste provokes immediate response—
to reject or repeat an experience.

Taste, as the basis of qualitative judgment of all human feelings and behavior, is a demonstrable discipline requiring that a felt response be parallel to a given thought or deed, so that the good one practices is also the good one feels.

When one learns to let the bad feel bad and the good feel good, ethical and aesthetic judgment becomes a reflex.

By recognizing rewarding patterns man learned to perceive goodness and beauty.
These qualities he refined into moral and aesthetic ideals that inspired and fulfilled his sense of order and spiritual needs.

There is no essential difference between moral values and good taste.
Both aim at the well being of humanity.
It is in the way the two concepts engage the mind that makes one more adaptable than the other.

While morality emphasizes abstention from doing specific things, taste permits responsible freedom to explore how circumstances modify the merits of any given thing, including taboo and sin.

Morality is a code of behavior that implies divine prescription and tends to overrule thought and modifying circumstances.

That this heaven-oriented set of rules by which a "good person" lives parallels good taste should not be surprising.

As any "divinely inspired" virtue must have had a practical, mundane origin, so morality must be a formal outgrowth of a system designed to encourage social harmony through controlled behavior that promoted survival and quality of life.

In a rapidly changing world, growing ever more complex, moral rules do not easily adapt to changing relationships. A nude body may be a glorious symbol of innocent beauty or a lewd object debasing a noble creature. Volunteering a truth may be a virtuous deed or a cruel intent to hurt or humiliate a person without a redeeming purpose.

Awareness of the consequences of one's actions and the ability to feel with another person are intrinsic judgments that guide our spontaneous responses in the use of taste as a guide to proper behavior.

Creativity

Creative involvement of body and mind is a spiritual experience that brings heaven to earth and the awareness of a supreme order into every humble task one performs.

Creativity is applied intelligence and imagination. It is a health-seeking response of body and mind to eliminate monotony and animate life, to relieve stress and other discomforts by externalizing one's sense of order and beauty.
The primary force behind creative activities is the need to bring into harmony the incidental dissonances of daily living.

All purposeful, satisfying, human endeavors are creative and expressive, in varying degrees. A purposeful endeavor is the pleasurable release of expressive energy resulting from the negative tension of pain, boredom and anxiety or the positive exuberance derived from intense appreciation of life.

The degree of imbalance or irritability in a person may well be the measure of one's potential creative power. The so called "talent" is that extra energy triggered by irritation or exuberance that seeks a medium of expression to constructively channel or transform it into a pleasurable experience. This natural inclination, to exercise self-therapy through self expression, is the basic force of creativity.

A forceful expression may at times produce art—a structured work with sufficient emotional depth and clarity to compel another to respond with the same gratification that rewarded the artist. However, art is a relatively rare occurrence while creativity, as the active manifestation of intelligence and imagination, is common and universal.

Art and self-expression are terms often used by dishonest, so-called artists and critics to justify abuses of artistic freedom in their pretentious claims to artistry with banal works that aim at shocking the viewers more than enriching their aesthetic experience.

To be sure self-expression is an element of art,
but self-expression in itself is not art.

The act of externalizing one's responses to the world ranges from spontaneous, simple exclamations to corrective compensation for the ever-recurring imbalances of the human organism.
Some people pray to offset fear or desperation. Others rage to allay frustration, and still others transform irritation into constructive work. Though this phenomenon is universal, one's specific experience is intensely personal and self-serving in maintaining equilibrium in one's life.

Art is of man
and never neutral.

Born of chaos
and the need to harmonize;
Born of boredom
and the need to vitalize;
Born of complexity
and the need to clarify;
Born of ambiguity
and the need to emphasize;
Born of ideas
and the need to visualize;
Born of discontent
and the need to transform it;
Born of pain
and the need to alleviate it;
Born of pleasure
and the need to intensify it;
Born of love
and the need to express it.

New ideas arise in the mind much the same way among artists, inventors, writers and scientists.

All creative people are intuitive souls who share an informal attitude and personal mode of exploring new relationships of knowledge.

Creative people in all disciplines synthesize what they know and feel in the calm appreciation of life.

Contemplation of life's experience is the incubation of knowledge that precedes the outflow of creative impulses: the pressing feeling of a pregnant mind that insists on externalizing something real that it cannot yet explain, the spontaneous insight of a new idea or vision, born of passion and culminating in the exuberance of discovery.

Each person, in his own medium, coaxes a vague concept out into the open as a mother gives birth to a viable body that has been forming for months. And like a mother, the scientist and the artist rear their new child in the lab and in the studio until it stands alone and is sufficiently formed to be used and enjoyed by others.

Artistic achievement is only an intensified form of common expression in everyday life.

As the telescope and the microscope magnify and bring into focus the physical world, so art intensifies experience to give a clearer vision of human aspiration, fulfillment and appreciation of sensuous and spiritual life.

Art, as the culmination of sensitive intelligence that cultivates beauty of mind and matter, is the creative blending of functional forms with the essence of the human soul that gives unity to purpose and meaning.

The practice of equating creativity with exceptional levels of inventiveness makes the word too exclusive. It downplays the importance of this basic human quality in its universal application in everyday life.

To be creative is not a choice. It is an integral part of a reflective mind. One can only choose to stifle or enhance it.

Creative self-expression is an important human attribute even without reference to art or talent. One should sing to celebrate his feelings.
This simple, spontaneous act should not become a conscious effort to show off a marketable skill. It should be a sincere manifestation of a state of mind, wanting to vocalize elation or transform a melancholic mood into a healing expression of celebration.

Children should not be taught "art" with the expectation of becoming artists. They should be encouraged to be creative as an integral part of their natural development.

The practice of reducing every fulfilling human expression to career-oriented goals negates the ultimate fulfillment of one's quality of being.
The subordination of meaningful human experiences to the pursuit of mechanical means is a confirmation of the current confusion between the values of materialism and the spiritual ends of human existence.

*There is something innate in a child's preference
to push a crayon in orbit on a paper sky.
There is something basic in the mind
that brings a line around to enclose a circle.
As naturally as the tongue licks his upper lip,
a child discovers a conclusive shape that he may name
a person or thing and give visual entity to a felt idea.*

*There is something in the mind that wants to imitate God by
animating clay and stone or breathing musical life into a wooden flute.
An artist sees firsthand the coming together of lines and shadows,
the blending of sounds and colors into a unified organism
with its own integrity of life to which
nothing can be added or subtracted
without disturbing life itself.*

The range of creativity is an unbroken line from simple expressions to artistic achievement.
There is no valid standard by which one recognizes and determines a creative effort as art except by general acclamation and the test of time.

The most prolific eras of Fine Arts grew out of a rich background of folk art and folk participation in civil and religious projects.
Themes and inspirations for great symphonies emerged from deep-rooted folk tunes and songs that people sang for the pure Joy of singing.
Great sculptors grew out of the artisan ranks of jewelers and stone cutters.
The poet too is of the common people and writes of common things with uncommon simplicity.

Creative expression as the social medium of sharing experiences through storytelling, building cities, and making music together is the reinforcer and unifier of humanity.
The venting of physical and mental energy through dance and songs, the release of joy and pain through laughter and tears, are part of the shock-absorbing system that keeps the human soul on an even keel through the ups and downs of life.

The Circular Route of Life

It is ironic but reassuring the way man flies aloft and steps nimbly upon the Earth that holds him fast by the feet.

Man and his ideals progress in a circular pattern as nature revolves within its set limits that make death a condition for life and evil a pretext for goodness.
For every beginning nature prescribes an end.
For every end it promises a new beginning.

Man has no say on when or where to be born.
He has no choice on when to die.
He has no memory of a former life and no proof of the beyond.
From generation to generation, mankind retraces its steps in a predictable pattern driven by the same biological wants and spiritual aspirations.

Even as we spin with the world, man and cultures rise and fall like the passing of seasons. Thus, we perceive eternity in the recurring cycles of life. Thus, we perceive our world as our destiny and place of continuous arrival where life rests at night and awakens every morning to a new beginning.

As the world spins from night to day, humanity perceives life as an experience of contrasting duality. Good and bad, hot and cold, black and white are distinct experiences that contribute clarity and intensity to the dynamic unity of felt understanding.

Night and day are understood in juxtaposition to one another, though darkness without a light and brightness without a shadow are both blind.
We understand virtue because we know vice.
Even God needs to coexist with evil.

Life is a rhythmic pulsation of contrary forces. Like inhaling and exhaling, each action is a reaction to the other, both necessary to breathing and the survival of the organism that sustains the process.
One cannot remove from life those negatives that are an intrinsic part of life itself.
Happiness and spiritual harmony depend on the orchestration of the good and the bad into a higher synthesis of spiritual oneness.
Pain or sadness is not an entity that one can remove from life. It is a state of mind that a person overcomes with a good measure of goodness and creative compensation.

When the soup is too salty it is easier to add water than remove the salt.

Life is not a road to some other place.
To be alive is a condition of having arrived.

Life is characterized by consistent repetition of the same old things.
The sun rises in the east every morning and the seasons follow each other in the same sequence year after year.
People still eat, work and make love essentially as they did in primordial days. Originality usually entails old themes restated with renewed vitality in relation to current needs and applications.

I tell despairing students, "Your work is not a failure but merely unfinished." Life is, after all, a process of redoing the same things with enough creative compulsion to continually renew experience with variations and enrichment of the basic design of nature.

Repetition rather than change binds future and past to the present and gives continuity to life and history. Every step we take forward is also a step toward the past on our perennial circular path where past and future forever converge under our feet.

In all we do, we reassert the same aspiration of our predecessors, and in a real way confirm their presence in our own lives by performing their music and repeating their stories as a preamble to our own.

Man's attempts to rival God have by far exceeded the Tower of Babel, reached the moon and beyond, only to find a run-away universe that pushes God's domain ever further from human understanding.

God's code for its creative handiwork is as evident on Earth as it is in the infinite emptiness of the cosmos. For man to accept the world as the outer limits of his home, with all the benefits of mind and senses to appreciate the gift of life, is not too humbling a restriction.

The sense of union that man feels with nature and God need not have come apart when science proved that Earth is but a small planet revolving around a mediocre star that moves within a galaxy that moves within other galaxies within an infinite unknown. Science merely explores. It does not change laws or basic principles of nature.

Our new relationship to the expanding world has only changed the scale of the Godly embrace of a creation that contains worlds of self-embracing nature, down to its smallest denominator.

As we move about our flat world, within the limits of our senses, a domed sky moves along with us to reconfirm the principle that the center of an unlimited universe can be at any point of observation. The intuitive spiritual man was generally right in thinking of himself as the heir of his world, and now we may add, in the middle of God's universe.

Some people perceive life as a relay race where an individual runs his course of a lifetime, then hands over the baton to a fresh runner who will, in turn, try to hold or improve the position passed on to him. Others see life as an endless ladder on which one climbs only a few steps in a lifetime. But no matter at what point of the ladder one starts, or on whose back he reaches the starting point, taking one's own step is all that registers as personal experience.

As humanity runs the circular course that repeats itself from generation to generation, one realizes that the cumulative progress of society does not determine the degree of harmony in life or its appreciation.

Appreciation and quality of experience are relative terms of personal perception. Whatever knowledge, skills and material convenience one is born into becomes a basic expectation—a mere point of departure. Though a soul could thrive on much less than our society prescribes, we cannot be happy with less than we already have. Those in the past who had less were no less happy than we are today. What we know merely ups the ante for what we need to know to sustain happiness.

Scope and sense of fulfillment in life does not depend on how much we know, but rather, on how well we enjoy the process of learning and how well we integrate and exercise what we already know.

From birth to death any direction is forward whether it is guided by wisdom or folly. Orientation is a state of mind. One person may think of going to... and another think of coming from... while both are walking in the same direction.

Progress or moving ahead is meaningless motion without a stable frame of reference to orient thought and qualify values.

Security and enrichment of the spirit require a stable society to sustain the humanizing process of home and family experience that personalizes love as a culminating experience of being.

Mere knowledge is no more rewarding than a book gathering dust on a shelf. Meaning is animated knowledge. Animation is the expression or creative application of what we know and feel.

Harmony qualifies life rather than quantitative knowledge.
Regardless of how much knowledge and refinement history passes on to us, each soul enters life in total innocence and departs in relative ignorance.

We have only a lifetime to balance the acquiring of skills and material needs with the rewarding experience of spirit that gives unity and energy to our expressions of love and our appreciation for life.

Cornerstone - Granite

Afterword

The freedom I have exercised in expressing my personal outlook on life rests on the premise that people share a common humanity and that in all honest expression there is a bit of the universal.

I assume that anything I say has been said by others in their own way and time, and as a fellow traveler in our circular route of life I have no choice but to think my own thoughts and dream my own dreams, no matter how many others have enjoyed doing the same before me.

In my endeavor to be:
I seek to fully engage mind and body and let my words and spirit achieve unity in what my hands touch and shape.
I seek no final truth any more than I crave to be permanently satiated.
I am thankful for my recurring appetites.
I take energy from life's challenges and personal discoveries.
I find security in the inexhaustibility of the unknown.

Meteorite - Limestone

Photographs and Sculptures

The photographs within the text of this book were selected from a photographic project undertaken by the author—a search for sculptural shapes created by the natural abrasion of wind and rain on limestone cliffs and caves near his native town in Italy.

The two sculptures on previous pages, by the author, share an organic affinity with shapes formed by natural forces.